THE GREAT COOKS' GUIDE TO

America's leading food authorities share their home-tested
recipes and expertise on cooking equipment and techniques

THE GREAT COOKS' GUIDE TO

Salads

A BEARD GLASER WOLF BOOK

RANDOM HOUSE, NEW YORK

Book Design by Milton Glaser, Inc.

Cover Photograph by Richard Jeffery

Copyright © 1977 by Morris Propp
All rights reserved under International and Pan-American
Copyright Conventions. Published in the United States by
Random House, Inc., New York, and simultaneously in
Canada by Random House of Canada Limited, Toronto.

Library of Congress Cataloguing in Publication Data
Main entry under title:

The Great Cooks' Guide to Salads.
1. Salads.
TX807.G75   1977   641.8′3   77-5973
ISBN: 394-73423-8

Manufactured in the United States of America
2 4 6 8 9 7 5 3

We have gathered together some of the great cooks in this country to share their recipes—and their expertise—with you. As you read the recipes, you will find that in certain cases techniques will vary. This is as it should be: cooking is a highly individual art, and our experts have arrived at their own personal methods through years of experience in the kitchen.

THE EDITORS

Contents

GREEN SALADS

VEGETABLE SALADS

LEGUME AND RICE SALADS

SEAFOOD SALADS

MEAT, POULTRY AND CHEESE SALADS

FRUIT SALADS

According to eighteenth-century gastronome Jean Anthelme Brillat-Savarin, a salad "freshens without enfeebling and fortifies without irritating."

Salads

On that distant day when Early Man (or Woman) snatched up a handful of wild greens, took a tentative munch and exclaimed "Wow!" the salad took its niche in the world's cuisine. Lettuce, in fact, was so appreciated by ancient Egyptians that they offered it to their fertility god Min, in honor of its supposed aphrodisiac qualities. The Romans showed a touching faith in greenery, too. They ate watercress with vinegar to cure mental ailments.

Our claims to salad's benefits may be less extravagant (or wishful) but we eat it in every form imaginable and serve it as any course of a meal, literally from soup to nuts. What is *gazpacho,* the summer blend of tomatoes, cucumbers and bell peppers, but soup in the form of salad? And the Chinese combination of crisp asparagus tips marinated in garlic and soy sauce and sprinkled with chopped walnuts is one of spring's delights. Salads come to the table as appetizers, main courses and desserts. *Larousse Gastronomique,* the definitive encyclopedia on the art of cooking, tersely describes salads as "dishes made up of herbs, plants, vegetables, eggs, meat and fish, seasoned with oil, vinegar, salt and pepper, with or without other ingredients." If the "other ingredients" include gelatin for aspics and fruit, that includes almost everything!

Probably the most popular type of salad, basic to our way of eating, is the tossed green salad. It clears the palate and aids the digestion, satisfies the craving for something slightly tart in the middle of a meal, and is blessed and savored by the weight-and-nutrition-conscious. At its simplest, a tossed salad consists only of greens, oil and vinegar, complementing each other in harmonious balance. But combinations and additions are endless—half a hundred varieties of salad greens, raw vegetables, herbs, cheese, cream and yogurt. From east to west the shopper finds an assortment of salad makings that would have astonished our forebears. Great grandma's summer choice was strictly limited, and winter salads, aside from cabbage, consisted of pickles and storable roots. Mrs. Bowdich (author of *Confidential Chats with Mothers*) wrote her cookbook, *New-Vegetarian-Dishes,* in 1892. She lists only nine salads, not one containing lettuce. How would Mrs. Bowdich cope in a market today, choosing among tender Boston, crisp-textured romaine and head lettuce, chicories and endives, red-tinged oakleaf, the soft and glorious Bibb, sharp cress or pungent rocket? (Rocket is a peppery plant called *ruchetta* in Italy and *roka* in Greece, but it can usually be found under the strictly Italian-American name of *arugula* in markets across the country.)

1

Buying Fresh Ingredients: Many instructions on salad making begin by advising the shopper to buy only the freshest produce available; presumably the authors are under the impression that we must be held back by the arm to keep us from grabbing up tired, wilted, moulting lettuce and limp and flabby vegetables. Nonsense! Of course we buy the best the market has to offer. If all the lettuce is blighted but the vegetables look good, we shift gears and opt for a cucumber and dill salad, or perhaps one of blanched zucchini dressed with oil, lemon, parsley and garlic.

Storage: When it comes to storing produce, opinions differ. However, we believe that the best policy is to store greens and fresh vegetables unwashed, packed loosely into plastic bags and kept in the crisper of the refrigerator, until shortly before use. This is because moisture invites mold and hastens deterioration. To save space, strip off any blemished leaves. If carrots come with their feathery tops attached, cut them off; they will continue to draw nourishment from the roots.

There are a few simple rules for making a salad. None of them is complicated, but they must be observed in turn if the salad is to be perfect. The steps are: washing, drying, chilling and dressing.

Washing: Since nothing is nastier than a sandy salad, the ingredients must be scrupulously clean. Not all greens get the same treatment—the hardier varieties of lettuce such as romaine, endive or chicory may be rinsed under the faucet; but a jet of water could bruise the tender leaves of Bibb or baby leaf lettuce. Separate the leaves carefully, and agitate them gently in several changes of water until no particles of grit remain. Cleaning fresh spinach often requires a saint-like patience as pails of sand fill up the sink, but the end result is worth the effort. For iceberg lettuce, core out the solid stem, hold the head upside-down under the tap, and let the water pressure spread and wash the leaves.

Drying: The greens must be dried—really dried—if the dressing is to cling to them, and this can be awfully tedious. You may shake the leaves in a colander or twirl them in a basket with an up-and-over windmill motion of the arm, then lay them between layers of linen, terry cloth or paper towels, patting gently and changing the sopping towels when necessary. In the last few years lettuce dryers have come on the market. They work on the principle of centrifugal force: in most models the torn greens are placed in an inner basket with large perforations. A crank, a knob (the Mouli plastic spin-dryer is equipped with this) or the pull-cord arrangement found on outboard motors causes the basket to spin, forcing water out where it is caught by the solid outer basket. The greens are dry and so is the kitchen. A marvelous, marvelous invention! Worth every penny! In fact, the greens are so dry they need only be placed in a plastic bag with a paper towel (to absorb the last vestiges of moisture) and chilled until they are ready to be used.

Salad Bowls: Which brings us to the choice of salad bowl. Many salad

2

Metal Spin-Dryer. This spin-dryer has taken the traditional mesh salad basket one step further, with the addition of a spin-dry mechanism that works on the same principle as a child's top.

Plastic Spin-Dryer. A slightly more space-aged item, this unbreakable polypropylene salad dryer is composed of two baskets — an outer one to catch the spun-off water, and an inner one to hold the greens. The top contains the gear mechanism that spins the inner basket.

Glass Salad Bowl. One of the best materials in which to mix and serve salads is glass: it is easily cleaned (unlike plastic) and will not retain the potentially undesirable flavors of previous salads (unlike wood).

lovers believe that salad made in a wooden bowl might as well have been made in an old rowboat. True, an unvarnished wooden bowl takes on a glorious patina with each application of salad oil. It *looks* great. But the oil turns rancid (unless the bowl is washed, in which case the next salad may taste of wet wood); and if the bowl is rubbed with garlic as many cookbooks insist, that may turn rancid, too. In a glass or ceramic bowl, each salad starts life afresh, unhaunted by last week's roquefort dressing.

Tossing the Salad: Whatever the choice of bowl, it should be large enough so that the tosser has enough room to turn the ingredients freely. A wide, shallow bowl is preferable to a high-sided one; you have more control over the operation. In France there is an old saying that a young girl who has learned to toss a salad deftly and prettily without scattering a leaf is "ready for marriage." Mademoiselle makes sure that the bowl is no more than half full. French salad-lore also states that twenty tosses are sufficient to coat each leaf. More would be exaggeration; less, laziness. Some people feel that the only way to toss a salad properly is with bare hands. That obviously won't work for those who like the threatrics of dressing the salad at the table. For them, James Beard's wooden "salad hands" achieve the effect without the mess.

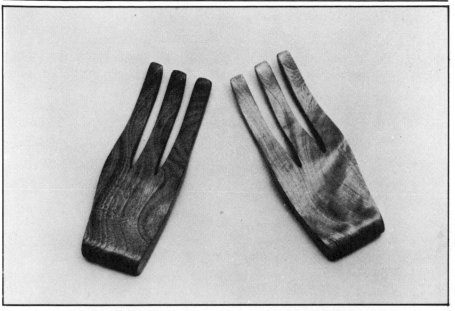

James Beard's Wooden Salad Hands. James Beard says: "My specially made salad hands…get down to the bottom and bring up just the right amount of dressing, fold the ingredients neatly and, most importantly, they're perfect for serving at the table."

Dressing: The dressing may be prepared in advance, but it should not be added to the salad until just before serving: vinegar and salt break down lettuce structure, leeching out both water and vitamin content. If you like, mix the dressing in the bowl. The classic formula for a vinaigrette is three parts of oil to one of vinegar, though to many palates five to one is nearer the mark. Depending on the composition of the salad, you may want to add mustard, salad herbs and garlic. Some dissolve a small amount of salt in the vinegar before adding the oil, others prefer to salt the salad only after it is served. To add only a hint of garlic, rub a crust of stale bread with a split clove of garlic and toss it with the salad. The crust, called a *chapon,* is removed before serving. It makes a tasty tidbit, if not an elegant one. If you like a lot of garlic, or are making a lot of dressing, purée the garlic through a press into the dressing, then strain. Add a few grindings of fresh pepper from a peppermill just before tossing; it gives a lot more zing than the tinned, pre-ground variety.

Salad Oils: We've talked of oil and vinegar—how simple that sounds! But even a partial listing of available oils indicates the complex wealth of choice available to the salad buff. Even olive oil has its complications. The

Peugeot Peppermill. Durable, stainless-steel peppermill mechanisms from Peugeot are housed in a number of different sizes and shapes, including this classic beechwood mill. Peugeot mills in any form enjoy a well-deserved reputation; and you really *can* adjust the grind!

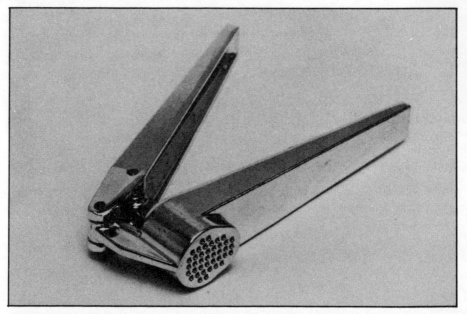

Aluminum Garlic Press. A sturdy press will rescue a salad from unpleasantly large pieces of garlic, providing instead a flavorful purée of the herb. The press section should fit the container tightly to force garlic through the holes efficiently.

Tinned-Steel Oil Can. If you've ever tried to pour small amounts of oil from a large can and then faced the problem of the inevitable drips, you will appreciate an oil storage can like this. The long narrow spout helps prevent drips, and the can holds a generous five cups.

lightest oil, the one that rises to the top after the first pressing of the finest olives, the French dignify by the curious title "extra virgin." This is the queen of oils—but not necessary or even desirable for every salad. Use it with Bibb or baby garden lettuce where its delicate flavor can be appreciated. More robust oils, green-gold pressings from Italian, Spanish or Greek olives, are suitable for heartier salads such as lentils or bulgur wheat, or crisp green beans with slivered Bermuda onion. After olive oil—in all its strengths and qualities—come a host of fine salad oils such as peanut, corn, soy bean, safflower, sesame (light from the Middle East, dark and aromatic from the Orient) and the increasingly rare walnut. Walnut oil is sold commercially at great cost, and, used without caution, is heavy and obtrusive. However, if you are lucky enough to dine with one of the last Provençales who still press their own oil from their own walnut groves . . . you'll remember that salad for the rest of your life!

Vinegars: There seem to be as many vinegars as there are oils. Red and white wine, cider, grain, and rice vinegars are best known. The list goes on with Chinese black and red vinegars, and an array of spiced vinegars. Of course, many people prefer to substitute lemon juice for vinegar, or to add it to a dressing. Herbs steeped in vinegar for a few weeks give off their flavors—the essence is captured and held for years to come. If you have an herb garden, experiment with different combinations; flavored vinegars make fine Christmas presents. Why not make your own wine vinegar? It's possible to have a constant supply of superior wine vinegar with a barrel and a "mother" from the California wine country. Mother of vinegar is the agent that converts alcohol to vinegar; "mother" is to vinegar as starter is to sourdough bread. You can adjust the vinegar to your taste, strong or mild. The nine-inch-long, brass-hooped barrel is made of sturdy Arkansas oak. To order a "mother," a barrel and its stand, write to: Franjoh Cellars, P.O. Box 7462, Stockton, California 95207.

Composed Salads: Variations of the tossed salad grow into a meal with many or a few additions. These are called "composed" salads. In the south of France, potatoes, tomatoes, hard-cooked eggs, anchovies, tuna, and black olives join lettuce to make *salade Niçoise.* In America, we add strips of ham, cheese and chicken to lettuce and call it chef's salad. No one can give authorship to these concoctions—they just grew, logically, from ingredients that go well together. But it took a sort of genius, Caesar Cardini, to invent the salad that bears his name. Who in the ordinary run of things would think that romaine lettuce, coddled eggs, Parmesan cheese, lemon juice and garlicy bits of bread could have anything to do with each other? Much less taste splendid? Caesar did, and he created a classic.

Salads needn't contain lettuce to qualify as such. In fact, many main-course salads don't use lettuce at all. Based on pasta, rice, potatoes or legumes, these salads are inexpensive, rib-sticking and earthy. Unfortunately, they are usually reserved for the family. But just because a dish is economical is no reason *not* to serve it to company. One well-heeled Chicago hostess makes a point of serving hearty bean and lentil salads to her even richer guests. "They, poor dears, dine out so much they're never offered home-style food," she says. "Many of them fancy themselves connoisseurs of wine and *grande cuisine,* but they've no idea how delicious *bourgeoise* cooking is. They're *overwhelmed!"*

Aspics: Aspics are another variation on the salad, and for transforming almost anything into a party dish, nothing beats these glistening molds. An aspic looks so sophisticated, but all it really demands is time. Molded salads can dazzle as a first course—try a whole striped bass *en gelée,* enclosed in a film of aspic—or they can be simple, ingenious foils for meat or poultry, like molded horseradish salad served with cold roast beef. In the Southwest and the Midwest, molded lime gelatin salad is the standby of the ladies' lunch. It can be artificial tasting and cloying, or refreshingly sweet and sour, depending on the recipe and the sensitivity of the cook.

Salad is good enough for royalty; Queen Elizabeth lunches on lobster and champagne salad each year in the Royal Enclosure at Ascot. You don't need a royal occasion to enjoy salad. Enjoy it every day of the year!

Plastic Lemon Squeezer. Many people use lemon juice instead of vinegar in salad dressings. This no-nonsense lemon squeezer will squeeze, strain and hold up to three cups of juice. The juice container has a handle, a pour spout and a non-skid rubber grip on the bottom.

Franjoh Vinegar Barrel. A sturdy oak cask from California contains everything you need to make your own wine vinegar — including the all-important "mother." By replenishing the wine as you use the vinegar, you will always have a fresh supply of homemade vinegar on hand.

Green Salads

MIXED "SALADE LORETTE"

Nicola Zanghi

4 servings

Dressing:
⅔ CUP OLIVE OIL
⅓ CUP WINE VINEGAR
1 TEASPOON MINCED SHALLOTS
1 EGG YOLK
1 TEASPOON SALT
1 TEASPOON WORCESTERSHIRE
    SAUCE
½ TEASPOON DRIED TARRAGON,
    OR 2 TEASPOONS CHOPPED
    FRESH TARRAGON, IF AVAILABLE
DASH TABASCO OR HOT SAUCE
1 TEASPOON DIJON-STYLE
    MUSTARD

Other Ingredients:
2 HEADS BELGIAN ENDIVE
1 BUNCH ARUGULA (ROCKET) OR
    WATERCRESS, WELL-WASHED
2 CUPS SLICED BEETS
1½ CUPS SLICED RAW
    MUSHROOMS
1 CAN HEARTS OF PALM, DRAINED
1½ CUPS SHELLED WALNUTS
1 CUP RED ITALIAN ONIONS,
    SLICED INTO RINGS
¼ CUP CHOPPED PARSLEY
FRESHLY GROUND BLACK PEPPER
    TO TASTE

1. Whisk all the ingredients for the dressing one day in advance so that the flavors can develop.

2. Preheat the oven to 350 F. and toast the walnuts for 15 minutes. Remove and cool them.

3. Separate the endive leaves and wash and dry them. Place the leaves on plates or in salad bowls. Arrange the arugula or watercress on top of the endive. Place the sliced beets, mushrooms, hearts of palm, walnuts, and onion rings on top of the greens. Sprinkle chopped parsley on the salad. Pepper generously.

4. Serve the dressing at the table.

ROMAINE LETTUCE SALAD, CHINESE STYLE

Grace Zia Chu

4 servings

1 HEAD ROMAINE LETTUCE
¼ CUP FINELY SHREDDED RED
   CABBAGE
1 TABLESPOON CHOPPED SCALLION
   (GREEN PART ONLY)
2 TABLESPOONS LIGHT SOY SAUCE
3 TABLESPOONS VEGETABLE OIL
1 TABLESPOON TARRAGON
   VINEGAR
2 TABLESPOONS LEMON JUICE

1. Slice the washed and dried lettuce into shreds (about 3 cups). Mix it with the red cabbage and scallion.

2. Mix the soy sauce, vegetable oil, tarragon vinegar and lemon juice in a bowl and let stand for 10 minutes.

3. Pour the dressing over the salad. Chill for a few minutes.

LETTUCE WITH JAPANESE PEANUT SALAD DRESSING

Paula J. Buchholz

¾ cup dressing

This flavorful mixture really dresses up shredded iceberg lettuce and is also wonderful tossed with romaine.

¼ CUP SALAD OIL
3 TABLESPOONS RICE VINEGAR
2 TABLESPOONS CHOPPED DRY
   ROASTED PEANUTS
2 TABLESPOONS SUGAR
2 TABLESPOONS TOASTED SESAME
   SEEDS
3 SCALLIONS, THINLY SLICED
   (INCLUDING GREEN PART)
1 TEASPOON SALT
½ TEASPOON MONOSODIUM
   GLUTAMATE (OPTIONAL)
½ TEASPOON FRESHLY GROUND
   BLACK PEPPER

1. Combine all of the ingredients, mixing until they are well blended. Any extra dressing can be kept for several days in the refrigerator.

GREEN GODDESS SALAD

Paul Rubinstein

6 to 8 servings

1 HEAD ROMAINE LETTUCE
1 HEAD BOSTON LETTUCE
1 LARGE, JUST-RIPE AVOCADO
½ CUP MAYONNAISE
4 TABLESPOONS ANCHOVY PASTE
½ CUP SOUR CREAM
2 TABLESPOONS CHOPPED CHIVES
2 TABLESPOONS LEMON JUICE
2 TABLESPOONS TARRAGON
   VINEGAR
¼ CUP FRESH CHOPPED PARSLEY
¼ TEASPOON FRESHLY GROUND
   BLACK PEPPER
1 SMALL CLOVE GARLIC, CRUSHED

1. Separate the leaves of both the romaine and Boston lettuce, wash, tear them into 1-inch pieces, and pat dry on paper towels.

2. Peel and pit the avocado and cut it into thin slices.

3. Assemble the mayonnaise, anchovy paste, sour cream, chives, lemon juice, vinegar, parsley, pepper and garlic in a blender jar and blend at high speed for 30 seconds. If you don't have a blender, mix at high speed with an electric mixer until the dressing is smooth.

4. Place the lettuce leaves and sliced avocado in a salad serving bowl, pour on the dressing, toss well and serve.

ANCHOVY AND WALNUT GREEN WINTER SALAD

Diana Kennedy

4 servings

½ CUP CUBED WHOLE WHEAT
   BREAD FOR CROUTONS
1 LARGE CLOVE GARLIC, PEELED
⅓ CUP FENNEL ROOT, ROUGHLY
   CHOPPED
½ SMALL CAN OF ANCHOVY
   FILLETS
6 CUPS MIXED WINTER SALAD
   GREENS (ROMAINE LETTUCE
   AND/OR ANY OF THE
   FOLLOWING: CHICORY, ARUGULA
   (ROCKET), DANDELION LEAVES,
   SPINACH, WATERCRESS)

½ CUP WALNUT MEATS, BROKEN

Dressing:
1½ TEASPOONS DIJON-STYLE
   MUSTARD
4 TABLESPOONS OIL (PREFERABLY
   WALNUT OR A FRUITY OLIVE
   OIL)
2 TABLESPOONS LEMON JUICE OR
   SHERRY WINE VINEGAR
SALT
FRESHLY GROUND PEPPER

1. Dry the bread cubes in a 300 F. oven and let them brown slightly, without oil.

2. Crush the garlic in a salad bowl and rub it over the inner surface of the bowl and discard it. Add the dressing ingredients and beat well.

3. Toss the croutons and fennel briefly in the dressing.

4. Cut the anchovies into small pieces. Tear the greens into small pieces. Add these and the walnuts to the salad bowl and toss together in the dressing just before serving.

BIBB LETTUCE AND WATERCRESS SALAD WITH LEMON DRESSING

Paul Rubinstein

4 servings

1 HEAD BIBB LETTUCE
2 LARGE BUNCHES WATERCRESS

Dressing:
4 TABLESPOONS OLIVE OIL
2 TABLESPOONS LEMON JUICE
1½ TEASPOONS SUGAR
¼ TEASPOON FRESHLY GROUND
 BLACK PEPPER
¼ TEASPOON SALT
1 TEASPOON WORCESTERSHIRE
 SAUCE
2 TABLESPOONS CHOPPED FRESH
 CHIVES

1. Separate the lettuce leaves, wash, and tear them into 1-inch pieces; pat them dry on paper towels.

2. Trim the stems from the watercress, wash and pat the leaves dry with paper towels.

3. Assemble the dressing in the salad bowl. First put in the olive oil, lemon juice and sugar. Stir until the sugar dissolves and there is no gritty feel to the liquid. Add the pepper, salt and Worcestershire sauce and, last, sprinkle on the chopped chives.

4. Add the lettuce leaves and watercress to the salad bowl, toss thoroughly and serve.

SALAD IN THE STYLE OF PROVENCE

The Good Cooking School

6 servings

1 HEAD ROMAINE LETTUCE
2 HEADS ENDIVE
1 PACKAGE (10 OUNCES) FRESH
  SPINACH
¼ POUND FRESH MUSHROOMS
6 TO 8 TABLESPOONS OLIVE OIL
1½ TABLESPOON RED WINE
  VINEGAR

1 TEASPOON DIJON-STYLE
  MUSTARD
1 CLOVE GARLIC, CRUSHED
2 TABLESPOONS FINELY MINCED
  SCALLIONS
SALT
FRESHLY GROUND BLACK PEPPER

1. Separate the romaine and endive leaves. Trim the tough spinach stems. Wash and dry the greens. Wipe the mushrooms with damp paper towels.

2. Combine all remaining ingredients in a screw-top jar. Shake the jar vigorously until the dressing is smooth and well blended.

3. Pour the dressing into the bottom of a large salad bowl. Tear the greens into bite-sized pieces, slice the mushrooms and place them on top of the dressing in the bowl. Toss the salad just before serving.

LES JARDINS' WATERCRESS AND MUSHROOM SALAD

Harvey Steiman

2 to 4 servings

2 BUNCHES WATERCRESS
2 TABLESPOONS OLIVE OIL

Sauce:
1 TABLESPOON BUTTER
½ CUP FINELY CHOPPED
  SHALLOTS OR ONIONS
1 TABLESPOON FINELY CHOPPED
  CHIVES
½ TEASPOON SALT, OR MORE,
  TO TASTE

A FEW GRINDINGS OF BLACK
  PEPPER
JUICE OF 1 LEMON
1 TABLESPOON WINE VINEGAR
1 TEASPOON ANGOSTURA BITTERS
1 TEASPOON WORCESTERSHIRE
  SAUCE
1 CUP THINLY SLICED FRESH
  MUSHROOMS
DASH OF COGNAC

1. Rinse the watercress well, dry thoroughly and chill until ready to use.

2. The sauce is made in a skillet over moderate heat. A copper presentation skillet or chafing dish is ideal, but any heavy skillet will do fine. Have all the ingredients ready to go in small bowls or cups. Combine the oil and butter in the skillet. Heat until the butter foam subsides, then sauté the onions and chives until the onions become limp. Try not to brown them. Add the salt, pepper, lemon juice, vinegar, bitters and Worcestershire. Adjust the proportions to taste, adding more of any ingredient you wish.

3. When the sauce is seasoned to taste, add the mushrooms and simmer 2 or 3 minutes. Add cognac to the sauce and pour over the chilled cress.

4. Toss briefly to combine. Spoon the salad onto a chilled plate.

BIBB LETTUCE WITH
VINAIGRETTE DRESSING

The Good Cooking School

6 servings

4 TO 6 HEADS BIBB LETTUCE
2 TABLESPOONS CHOPPED
   PARSLEY

Dressing:
½ CUP OLIVE OR VEGETABLE OIL
   (OR ¼ CUP EACH)
1 TEASPOON SALT
½ TEASPOON FRESHLY GROUND
   PEPPER OR 1 TEASPOON DIJON-
   STYLE OR ENGLISH-STYLE
   MUSTARD
½ TEASPOON DRIED BASIL
2 TABLESPOONS WINE VINEGAR

1. Pull off and discard any bruised outer leaves on each head of lettuce. Quarter each trimmed head with a sharp knife, then carefully shave any brown from the root end of each section.

2. Hold each lettuce quarter under running water, gently spreading the leaves apart so that the running water bathes each leaf to remove all the sand. Drain and dry gently with paper towels and refrigerate until serving time.

3. Combine all ingredients but the vinegar and mix well. Add vinegar to taste. Stir well.

4. Place the lettuce in a salad bowl, sprinkle it with parsley and toss with enough dressing to coat each leaf.

SALAD WITH CREAM DRESSING
(SALADE À LA CRÈME)

The Good Cooking School

6 servings

This dressing is particularly good with tender salad greens such as Bibb, Boston and oak leaf lettuce. The dressing should be prepared ahead, but not tossed with the salad until serving time so that the greens will be crisp.

2 TO 3 HEADS BOSTON LETTUCE
   DEPENDING ON SIZE, OR 5 TO 6
   HEADS BIBB LETTUCE
½ TEASPOON SALT
½ TEASPOON FRESHLY GROUND
   WHITE PEPPER
4 TEASPOONS GOOD WINE
   VINEGAR
6 TABLESPOONS HEAVY CREAM
2 TABLESPOONS VEGETABLE OIL

1. Wash and thoroughly dry the lettuce. Tear it into bite-sized pieces. (Handle the lettuce gently to avoid bruising the leaves.) Arrange the lettuce in a large bowl and refrigerate until needed.

2. In a small bowl, combine the salt, pepper, vinegar and cream. Beat with a wire whisk for about 20 seconds. The mixture should have a foamy, creamy consistency. Add the oil and continue mixing. Refrigerate the dressing.

3. Just before serving, pour the dressing over the lettuce and toss gently.

Vegetable Salads

CAULIFLOWER WITH MUSTARD SEED BUTTER (CAULIFLOWER RAITA)

Michael Batterberry

4 to 6 servings

An Indian variation on salad, good with everything from elaborate curries to broiled hamburgers.

1 HEAD CAULIFLOWER (NOT TOO
   SMALL)
½ LEMON
1 TABLESPOON COARSE SALT PLUS
   1 TEASPOON
2 CUPS UNFLAVORED YOGURT
3 TABLESPOONS MUSTARD SEEDS
6 TABLESPOONS CLARIFIED
   BUTTER

1. Cut the cauliflower into medium flowerets. With a small, sharp knife, trim the heavy skin from their stems.

2. Put the cauliflower into a large enameled pan with cold water to barely cover, and add the juice of half a lemon. Bring to a boil, sprinkle with a tablespoon of coarse salt and simmer for 4 to 5 minutes. Drain immediately and thoroughly.

3. Beat the yogurt with a teaspoon of salt until creamily smooth.

4. Toss the cooled, dry cauliflower in the yogurt and refrigerate.

5. In a small, heavy enameled cast-iron pot with a cover, fry the mustard seeds over high heat in clarified butter. When you begin to hear popping and spattering sounds, count to 50 and remove from the heat. Do not lift the lid for another 5 minutes.

6. Drizzle the butter-mustard seed mixture over the cauliflower and yogurt and swirl together lightly with a wooden spoon. Do not overmix—this *raita* should have a streaky appearance.

NEW POTATO, JERUSALEM ARTICHOKE AND KOHLRABI SALAD (SALADE DESTOUCHES)

Raymond Sokolov

4 servings

10 NEW POTATOES, BOILED IN THEIR SKINS UNTIL JUST TENDER
5 RAW JERUSALEM ARTICHOKES, PEELED AND SLICED
3 RAW KOHLRABIS, PEELED AND SLICED
1 GREEN PEPPER, SEEDED AND DICED

½ CUP PEANUT OIL
1 TABLESPOON VINEGAR
¼ CUP DRY RED WINE
1 TABLESPOON MINCED ONION
2 TABLESPOONS CHOPPED FRESH CHIVES, PARSLEY, CHERVIL OR TARRAGON

1. Remove the skins from the potatoes. Let the potatoes cool, then slice them thin.

2. Just before serving, mix together all the ingredients. Toss lightly and serve.

POTATO AND MUSSEL SALAD

Carol Cutler

4 to 5 servings

In his play, *Francillon,* the younger Alexandre Dumas went on at great length describing this salad. Dumas, of course, glamorized it with truffles and champagne. The following version is more down-to-earth, but delicately delicious.

Potatoes:
2 POUNDS NEW POTATOES
2 CUPS CHICKEN BROTH
1 CUP WATER
CELERY LEAVES FROM TWO RIBS
1 CUP DRY WHITE WINE, AT ROOM TEMPERATURE

Dressing:
6 TABLESPOONS OLIVE OIL
2 TABLESPOONS WINE VINEGAR
SALT
PEPPER

¼ TEASPOON BASIL
¼ TEASPOON ROSEMARY
½ TEASPOON TARRAGON
¼ TEASPOON DRY MUSTARD

Mussels:
3 POUNDS MUSSELS (OR LITTLE NECK CLAMS)
½ LEMON
LETTUCE LEAVES FOR GARNISH
¼ POUND COOKED SHRIMP (OPTIONAL)

1. Scrub the potatoes well. Do not peel them. Put the potatoes in a small pot with the chicken broth and water and one sprig of celery leaves. Bring to a boil and simmer until the potatoes are soft, but not mushy, about 25 minutes.

2. Drain off the water, but reserve 1 cup.

3. While the potatoes are cooking, beat together all the ingredients for the dressing.

4. As soon as you can handle the potatoes (holding the hot potatoes with paper towels helps a lot), peel and cut them into slices about ¼ -inch thick.

5. Place the slices in a mixing bowl. Immediately pour ⅓ cup of the white wine over the potatoes, mix gently and cover. Let stand for 10 minutes.

6. Pour the dressing over the potatoes, mix gently again, cover and set aside.

7. Scrub the mussels well and put them in a deep pot with the cup of reserved potato water, plus the remaining ⅔ cup wine and the remaining celery sprig. Squeeze in the lemon juice and toss in the lemon shell as well. Cover, bring to a boil over high heat and cook until the mussel shells open, usually just a few minutes. Cool, then remove the mussels from the shells. (You may reserve the liquid for soup.)

8. Reserve 3 or 4 mussels to garnish the salad and add the rest to the potatoes. Mix again carefully and leave at room temperature, covered, for 1 hour.

9. Refrigerate for at least 2 hours.

10. To serve, arrange a bed of lettuce leaves on a serving platter, mound the salad in the center and arrange the reserved mussels on top. If shrimp are also used for decoration, make a circle of them around the mussels.

POTATO AND APPLE SALAD

Helen McCully

4 to 6 servings

2 CUPS COOKED DICED POTATOES
2 CUPS CORED AND FINELY DICED
  RED DELICIOUS APPLES
½ SMALL YELLOW ONION, PEELED
  AND MINCED
½ CUP MAYONNAISE (SEE NOTE
  BELOW)
SALT
FRESHLY GROUND WHITE PEPPER
BIBB LETTUCE

1. Combine all the ingredients except the lettuce and mix with enough mayonnaise to hold the mixture together. Season to taste with salt and pepper.

2. Place in a salad bowl with a garland of Bibb lettuce leaves. Very good, indeed, with cold roast pork.

   Note: If you use commercial mayonnaise, add the strained juice of half a lemon.

RED, WHITE AND GREEN BEAN SALAD

Emanuel and Madeline Greenberg

6 servings

1½ POUNDS GREEN BEANS
1 MEDIUM-SIZED ONION, PEELED
   AND THINLY SLICED
1 4-OUNCE JAR OR CAN OF
   PIMIENTOS, DRAINED AND
   SLIVERED

Dressing:
¼ CUP OLIVE OIL
2 TABLESPOONS WINE VINEGAR
1 CLOVE GARLIC, CRUSHED
¼ TEASPOON DRIED BASIL
¼ TEASPOON DRIED OREGANO
¼ TEASPOON SUGAR
SALT TO TASTE
PEPPER TO TASTE

1. Trim the green beans and cut them into 1-inch lengths. Cook them in boiling salted water until just tender. Drain and cool.

2. Combine the beans with the onion and pimientos in a salad bowl.

3. Combine the remaining ingredients for the dressing and pour it over the vegetables. Toss well. Chill several hours and toss again before serving.

TUNISIAN MIXED SALAD

Paula Wolfert

4 to 6 servings

1 CUP PEELED, SEEDED AND DICED
   RIPE RED TOMATOES
1 CUP CHOPPED ONIONS
1 CUP SEEDED, DE-RIBBED AND
   DICED SWEET GREEN PEPPERS
1 TABLESPOON SEEDED AND
   FINELY CHOPPED HOT GREEN
   CHILI PEPPER
1 CUP PEELED, CORED AND DICED
   RAW GREEN APPLE

1½ TABLESPOONS VINEGAR
4½ TABLESPOONS OLIVE OIL
1 TABLESPOON PULVERIZED DRIED
   MINT LEAVES
SALT TO TASTE
FRESHLY GROUND BLACK PEPPER
   TO TASTE

1. Combine the tomatoes, onions, peppers, and apple in a serving bowl. Add the vinegar and oil and toss well.

2. Sprinkle with the pulverized mint, salt, and pepper. Mix thoroughly. Serve at room temperature.

TOMATOES FILLED WITH EGGPLANT AND ZUCCHINI

Elizabeth Colchie

6 servings

6 MEDIUM-SIZED TOMATOES
SALT FOR PREPARING THE
  TOMATOES
PEPPER FOR PREPARING THE
  TOMATOES
SUGAR FOR PREPARING THE
  TOMATOES
1½ TO 2 POUNDS EGGPLANT
  (APPROXIMATELY)

1 POUND ZUCCHINI
  (APPROXIMATELY)
2½ TEASPOONS SALT
1½ CUPS FINELY CHOPPED ONION
½ CUP OLIVE OIL
1 CLOVE GARLIC, MINCED
½ CUP FINELY MINCED PARSLEY
¼ CUP FINELY MINCED FRESH
  BASIL

1. Cut a ½-inch slice from the stem-ends of the tomatoes; scoop out and discard the seeds. Gently remove the pulp (I find a small melon baller works nicely); chop it and place it in a strainer over a bowl with a light sprinkling of salt, pepper and sugar. Lightly sprinkle the insides of the cases with salt, pepper and sugar. Turn the tomatoes upside-down and place them on a rack to drain.

2. Coarsely grate enough unpeeled eggplant to make about 4 cups; coarsely grate enough unpeeled zucchini to make about 3½ cups (use either a hand grater or a food processor). Toss the vegetables in a strainer with 2½ teaspoons salt and let them drain for about ½ hour. Press them down to remove excess liquid and dry them on paper towels.

3. Cook the onions in the olive oil in a large heavy skillet until just softened; add the eggplant and zucchini and cook the vegetables over moderate heat, tossing frequently, for about 5 minutes or until barely tender. Add the tomato pulp, cover and cook for a minute or two; add the garlic and toss the mixture for 2 to 3 minutes. If too much liquid remains, raise the heat and evaporate it. Taste, and season if necessary.

4. Combine the parsley and basil and sprinkle about a tablespoon in each tomato case. Fill the tomatoes with the vegetable mixture and place them in an oiled baking dish.

5. Bake the tomatoes in a preheated 450 F. oven for about 15 minutes or until the tomatoes are just soft, not broken. Let them cool, and sprinkle them with the remaining herb mixture. Serve at room temperature.

Note: These tomatoes are fine for picnics. Carry them in a big cupcake tin, with another inverted over the top. This will keep them from jiggling in transit.

AVOCADO AND MUSHROOM SALAD

Helen McCully

4 to 6 servings

⅓ CUP OLIVE OIL
1 TABLESPOON WINE VINEGAR
6 TO 8 SPRIGS MINCED PARSLEY
1 CLOVE GARLIC, CRUSHED,
　PEELED AND MINCED
JUICE OF 1 LEMON
SALT TO TASTE
FRESHLY GROUND PEPPER TO
　TASTE
2 AVOCADOS, PEELED AND SLICED
　THIN
½ POUND FRESH BUTTON
　MUSHROOMS, SLICED VERY THIN
PARSLEY FOR GARNISHING

1. With a wire whisk, beat together the oil, vinegar, minced parsley, garlic and lemon juice with salt and pepper to taste.

2. Pour the dressing over the avocados and mushrooms. Marinate for at least 1 hour. Arrange on individual plates and garnish with parsley.

HORSERADISH SALAD MOLD

Lyn Stallworth

6 servings

1 TABLESPOON SALAD OIL
2 CUPS BEEF STOCK, FRESH OR
　CANNED
1½ ENVELOPES UNFLAVORED
　GELATIN
¼ CUP SUGAR
1 TEASPOON SALT
2 TABLESPOONS FRESH LEMON
　JUICE
1 TEASPOON WORCESTERSHIRE
　SAUCE
1 4-OUNCE BOTTLE OF WHITE
　HORSERADISH, DRAINED IN A
　SIEVE AND SQUEEZED DRY

1. Brush the inside of a 2-cup mold with the oil; invert it on paper towels to drain.

2. Pour ½ cup of the beef stock into a small pan. Sprinkle it with the gelatin; let it soften for 3 minutes. Place the pan on low heat and stir constantly until the gelatin dissolves.

3. Add the remaining stock, sugar, salt, lemon juice and Worcestershire sauce. Continue to stir over low heat until the sugar dissolves.

4. Pour the gelatin mixture into a bowl; set it inside a larger bowl filled with crushed ice. Stir with a metal spoon until the gelatin thickens, then add the horseradish and mix well. Pour into the prepared mold and chill for 3 hours or until firm.

5. To unmold, run the blade of a knife around the rim of the mold to loosen the gelatin. Dip the bottom into hot water. Place an inverted serving plate over the mold, grasp the plate and mold together, and flip over.

GREEN BEAN AND WALNUT SALAD

Julie Dannenbaum

6 servings

2 POUNDS BABY GREEN BEANS
¾ CUP CHOPPED WALNUTS
½ CUP THINLY SLICED
  MUSHROOMS
SALT TO TASTE
FRESHLY GROUND BLACK PEPPER
  TO TASTE
1 TABLESPOON DIJON-STYLE
  MUSTARD
½ CUP WALNUT OIL, OR
  SUBSTITUTE OLIVE OIL
¼ CUP TARRAGON VINEGAR
2 TABLESPOONS CHOPPED FRESH
  PARSLEY

1. Bring a large kettle of salted water to a boil. Add the beans and boil, uncovered, 5 to 7 minutes or until they are just tender-crisp. Drain and refresh them in cold water. Dry the beans on a kitchen towel.

2. Place the beans in a salad bowl and sprinkle the walnuts and mushrooms over them.

3. Make a dressing of the salt, pepper, mustard, oil and vinegar and pour it over the salad.

4. Sprinkle with chopped parsley, toss and serve.

ZUCCHINI SALAD

Paula Wolfert

4 to 6 servings

1½ POUNDS SMALL FIRM
   ZUCCHINI (ABOUT 8), TRIMMED
1½ TEASPOONS CHOPPED GARLIC
1½ TEASPOONS GROUND CARAWAY
   SEED
3 TO 4 TABLESPOONS OLIVE OIL
1 TABLESPOON VINEGAR
SALT TO TASTE
FRESHLY GROUND PEPPER TO
   TASTE
CAYENNE PEPPER TO TASTE

1. Steam the zucchini until tender. Mash it to a purée.

2. Combine the zucchini with the garlic, caraway, olive oil, vinegar and seasonings, mixing well. Chill before serving.

RUSSIAN VEGETABLE SALAD
(SALADE RUSSE)

Ruth Spear

8 to 10 servings

2 10-OUNCE BOXES FROZEN PEAS,
   PARTLY DEFROSTED
2 10-OUNCE BOXES FROZEN BABY
   LIMA BEANS, PARTLY DEFROSTED
4 TO 6 CARROTS, DICED
4 TABLESPOONS FINELY MINCED
   ONION
2 TABLESPOONS LEMON JUICE
⅔ CUP MAYONNAISE
1 TEASPOON SALT
¼ TEASPOON WHITE PEPPER
2 TEASPOONS SUGAR
HANDFUL OF FINELY SNIPPED DILL

1. Bring 2 cups of salted water to a boil in a large pot. Add the peas and limas, a box at a time, allowing the water to return to the boil after each addition. Cover, lower the heat and cook the vegetables for 7 minutes. Drain the vegetables in a colander and run cold water over them. Allow the vegetables to cool while you make the sauce.

2. In a small bowl, beat the lemon juice into the mayonnaise with the salt, pepper and sugar.

3. Place the cooled peas and lima beans in a large mixing bowl. Add the diced carrots and minced onion. Pour the sauce over the vegetables and stir gently. Add the dill and mix again. Cover the salad tightly with plastic wrap and refrigerate it for 3 to 4 hours before serving.

POTATOES VINAIGRETTE

Julie Dannenbaum

4 servings

2 IDAHO POTATOES
1 TABLESPOON SALT
1 CUP WHITE VINEGAR
2 TABLESPOONS WINE VINEGAR
½ CUP OLIVE OR VEGETABLE
  OIL
SALT TO TASTE
FRESHLY CRACKED BLACK PEPPER
  TO TASTE
2 TABLESPOONS CHOPPED
  PARSLEY
2 TABLESPOONS CHOPPED CHIVES

1. Wash and peel the potatoes.

2. Slice the potatoes lengthwise, on a mandoline or with a vegetable cutter, the thickness of a quarter. They should be thinner than a kitchen match.

3. Bring a large kettle of water with 1 tablespoon of salt to the boil.

4. Add the potatoes and white vinegar and boil, uncovered, about 4 to 5 minutes. The potatoes should be tender-crisp.

5. Drain the potatoes and cool them in cold water. Dry them in a kitchen towel.

6. Put the potatoes in a salad bowl and pour over them the wine vinegar, oil, salt, pepper, parsley and chives. Toss.

   Note: This is a pleasant change from run-of-the-mill potato salad. Before the potatoes are dressed, they may be kept in the refrigerator for at least 10 days. They will not darken and can be added to other salads as a stretcher.

BUTTERMILK COLE SLAW

Florence Fabricant

6 servings

6 CUPS SHREDDED CABBAGE
¼ CUP PAPER-THIN ONION SLICES
1 CUP PAPER-THIN CARROT SLICES
   OR MATCHSTICKS
¾ CUP MAYONNAISE
¾ CUP BUTTERMILK
1 TEASPOON SALT
2 TABLESPOONS MINCED FRESH
   DILL

1. Mix the cabbage, onion and carrots in a large bowl.

2. Combine the mayonnaise, buttermilk and salt, stirring until smooth. Add this dressing to the vegetables and stir in the dill.

BEAN SPROUT SALAD

Carol Cutler

6 servings

For such a wispy looking thing, the bean sprout packs a lot of nutritional wallop. It is rich both in protein and vitamin C, and burdens you with very few calories. A whole pound of mung bean sprouts has only 160 calories. For this salad use soy bean, mung bean or lentil sprouts; alfalfa sprouts are too thin and delicate. Here is an unusual, crunchy and inexpensive luncheon main course, or a light-weight beginning to a dinner.

Dressing:
6 TABLESPOONS VEGETABLE OIL
2 TABLESPOONS SESAME SEED OIL
2 TABLESPOONS VINEGAR
JUICE OF 1 LEMON
2 TABLESPOONS SOY SAUCE
1 TEASPOON PREPARED MUSTARD
½ TEASPOON PAPRIKA
2 TABLESPOONS CHOPPED
   PIMIENTO
1 TEASPOON SALT
½ TEASPOON PEPPER

Other Ingredients:
1 POUND FRESH BEAN SPROUTS
¼ POUND FRESH MUSHROOMS
½ GREEN PEPPER, CHOPPED
   (ABOUT ½ CUP)
½ POUND DICED HAM OR
   CANADIAN BACON
CHERRY TOMATOES

1. Put all the ingredients for the dressing in a jar with a lid and shake well. All these steps can be prepared well in advance of serving time.

2. Place the sprouts in a colander, rinse them under cold running water and put them aside to drain. Rinse the mushrooms and let them stand to dry. Dice the ham.

3. When the salad is to be mixed and served, slice the mushrooms and chop the green pepper. Put the sprouts in a large mixing bowl and add the ham, mushrooms and green pepper. Pour the dressing over the salad and mix very well to distribute the dressing evenly. (I find that turning the vegetables with my own hands, or James Beard's wooden salad hands, works best.)

4. To serve, make a ring of the cherry tomatoes around the rim of the bowl. If the salad is put on individual plates before serving, place 1 or 2 cherry tomatoes as a garnish on each plate.

SWEET AND SOUR SMASHED RADISHES

Gloria Bley Miller

4 servings

3 BUNCHES RED RADISHES
1 TEASPOON SALT
1 GREEN PEPPER
2 TEASPOONS SOY SAUCE
1½ TABLESPOONS WHITE VINEGAR
1¼ TABLESPOONS BROWN SUGAR
½ TEASPOON CHINESE SESAME
   OIL (AVAILABLE IN ORIENTAL
   GROCERIES)

1. Wash and trim the radishes. Lay each on its side, then crush it lightly by pounding decisively once or twice with the side of a heavy knife or cleaver, or with the bottom of a heavy glass. (The radish should split open, but not break apart.)

2. Sprinkle them lightly with the salt. Let them stand for 10 minutes, then drain and transfer them to a bowl.

3. Meanwhile cut the green pepper in two, discard the seeds and sliver the pepper. Add to the radishes.

4. In a cup, combine the soy sauce, vinegar and sugar, blending well. Pour over the vegetables, tossing well to coat them.

5. Refrigerate, covered, only to chill (about 20 minutes). Sprinkle with the sesame oil, toss again and serve.

FRESH KOHLRABI SALAD

Grace Zia Chu

4 servings

2 OR 3 KOHLRABIS (ABOUT ½
POUND)
½ TEASPOON SALT
2 TABLESPOONS LIGHT SOY SAUCE
2 TABLESPOONS ORIENTAL SESAME
SEED OIL
½ TEASPOON SUGAR
1 TEASPOON CHINESE HOT PEPPER
OIL,* OR SUBSTITUTE 1
TEASPOON TABASCO OR HOT
SAUCE
2 TABLESPOONS SHREDDED
CARROT

1. Peel the kohlrabis carefully to remove all tough skin. Cut them first into slices and then into shreds, 1¼-by-¼-by-¼ inches. Place the shreds in a bowl and sprinkle them with salt. Let them stand for 25 minutes. At the end of the period, rinse the kohlrabi several times in cold water.

2. Mix the soy sauce, sesame seed oil, sugar and hot pepper oil in a bowl.

3. Shred the carrot and toss it with the kohlrabi. Pour the sauce over the vegetables and serve as a salad.

* These ingredients are available in Oriental groceries.

WHIPPED EGGPLANT SALAD
(MELITZANOSALATA)

Vilma Liacouras Chantiles

4 to 5 servings

Creamy and aromatic, *Melitzanosalata* is a wonderful challenge for the cook. Although easy to make and whip in a mixer or blender, the seasonings must be added artfully to please the cook's senses. The addition of tomatoes in Greece contrasts to the Asia Minor version, made without tomatoes. Try both variations.

1½ TO 2 POUNDS EGGPLANT
3 TO 4 CLOVES GARLIC, CRUSHED
1 TO 2 FRESH TOMATOES, PEELED
AND CHOPPED (OPTIONAL)
2 TO 3 TABLESPOONS MINCED
FRESH PARSLEY
1 TEASPOON DRIED OREGANO OR
SAVORY, CRUMBLED

SALT
FRESHLY GROUND PEPPER
⅓ TO ½ CUP FINE OLIVE OIL
6 TABLESPOONS RED WINE
VINEGAR (MORE IF NECESSARY)
PARSLEY FOR GARNISH
CHOPPED BLACK OLIVES FOR
GARNISH

1. Bake the eggplant in a moderate oven or hot ashes for about 45 minutes until softened. Peel off and discard the skins.

2. Chop the eggplant and combine it with the garlic, tomatoes (if using), parsley and oregano or savory in a mortar and pound for a few minutes until smooth. Or use an electric mixer, blender or food processor.

3. Beating steadily, season the mixture lightly with salt and pepper and begin adding the oil and vinegar alternately. Stop and taste for flavor. When thick, smooth and delicious, turn it into a bowl and chill.

4. When ready to serve, garnish the eggplant with parsley and black olives and serve cold with game, meat, or fish dishes as a salad or with crusty bread as an appetizer.

HOT ASPARAGUS SALAD

Ruth Spear

4 to 6 appetizer servings/3 to 4 main course servings

6 SLICES BACON, DICED
1 POUND ASPARAGUS, PREFERABLY
  MEDIUM-SIZED
1 CUP WINE VINEGAR
1 TABLESPOON SUGAR
¼ TEASPOON DRY MUSTARD
SALT
FRESHLY GROUND PEPPER
1 QUART SHREDDED LETTUCE
  LEAVES, BOSTON OR ROMAINE
2 HARD-COOKED EGGS, CHOPPED

1. Fry the bacon bits in a skillet until crisp. Remove them with a slotted spoon and reserve. Pour off all but 2 tablespoons of the drippings from the pan and discard.

2. Trim the asparagus and cut off the tips. Cut the stems on the diagonal into pieces 1-inch long. Add the stems to the skillet and cook them over medium-high heat, stirring constantly, until they are crisply tender and bright green, about 5 minutes. Add the tips and cook 1 minute longer.

3. Add the vinegar, sugar, mustard, salt and pepper to taste to the asparagus, then heat to the boiling point while stirring. Add the bacon bits.

4. Place the lettuce in a warmed bowl. Pour in the asparagus mixture. Sprinkle the salad with the chopped eggs, toss the ingredients together and serve warm.

CHINESE PICKLED CELERY AND CARROTS

Gloria Bley Miller

4 servings

2 CUPS CARROTS
2 CUPS CELERY
1½ TEASPOONS SALT
DASH OF PEPPER
1½ CUPS WHITE VINEGAR
3 TABLESPOONS SUGAR

1. Scrape or peel the carrots, then quarter and cut them into 2-inch sections. Trim the celery and cut it into 2-inch sections.

2. Bring the water to a rolling boil. Add ½ teaspoon of the salt, then the carrots and parboil them to soften slightly (about 3 minutes). Drain them in a sieve or colander. Cool at once under cold running water.

3. Bring fresh water to a rolling boil. Add another ½ teaspoon of salt, then the celery sections. Parboil to soften them slightly (about 2 minutes). Drain in a sieve or colander. Cool at once under cold running water.

4. Combine the vegetables and sprinkle them with the remaining ½ teaspoon of salt and the pepper. Transfer them to a jar or crock.

5. Bring the vinegar to a boil, then stir in the sugar to dissolve it. Pour it over the vegetables.

6. Cover the jar and shake well. Refrigerate overnight. Shake from time to time.

7. To serve, shake the jar well several times, then drain and discard the vinegar.

MOROCCAN RADISH AND ORANGE SALAD

Paula Wolfert

4 to 6 appetizer servings

2 TO 3 BUNCHES LONG OR ROUND
  RED RADISHES
2 TABLESPOONS SUGAR
JUICE OF 1 LEMON
1 TABLESPOON ORANGE-FLOWER
  WATER
SALT TO TASTE
2 NAVEL ORANGES, PEELED AND
  SECTIONED
CINNAMON

1. Wash and trim the radishes. Place them in a blender jar or processor and "grate" by turning the machine off and on. *Do not purée.*

2. Remove and drain off excess liquid. Place the grated radishes in a serving

dish and sprinkle them with the sugar, lemon juice, perfumed water and salt. Toss lightly and chill.

3. Just before serving, mix the orange sections with the grated radishes. Dust lightly with cinnamon and serve at once.

BELL PEPPER SALAD

Jeanne Lesem

2 salad servings/4 appetizer servings

2 LARGE GREEN OR RED BELL PEPPERS, OR ONE OF EACH
⅓ CUP RED ONION OR MILD YELLOW ONION, FINELY CHOPPED
1 TEASPOON GRATED OR THINLY SLIVERED CRYSTALLIZED GINGER OR ½ TEASPOON PEELED, FINELY GRATED FRESH GINGER ROOT

⅛ TEASPOON SALT
LIGHT SPRINKLING OF FRESHLY GROUND BLACK PEPPER
1 TEASPOON RED WINE VINEGAR OR WHITE WINE OR CIDER VINEGAR
½ TEASPOON DRY SHERRY

1. Halve the peppers lengthwise and place them, cut side down, on a foil-lined broiler tray as close to the heat source as possible. Broil 5 to 15 minutes, or until most of the skin turns black and the peppers begin to soften. Preheating the broiler is not necessary.

2. While the peppers broil, mix the onion, ginger, salt, pepper, vinegar and sherry in a small bowl. Beat vigorously with a small fork or wire whip, and set aside.

3. Remove the pepper halves to a small brown paper bag, twist shut, and let stand 5 minutes for further "cooking." Then remove one piece at a time with tongs and hold it under cold running water until cool enough to handle.

4. Peel, seed and remove the membranes of the peppers. Cut the peppers into ¼ -inch-wide strips or chop them coarsely, and mix with the dressing. Let stand at room temperature at least 1 hour, stirring occasionally. Serve at room temperature. If you want to hold the salad for a longer period, refrigerate it tightly covered, and return it to room temperature about 1½ hours before serving.

GREEN PEA AND PEANUT SALAD

Jane Moulton

6 servings

⅓ CUP SOUR CREAM
1 TABLESPOON MAYONNAISE
1 TEASPOON WORCESTERSHIRE
 SAUCE
¼ TEASPOON CURRY POWDER
1 10-OUNCE PACKAGE FROZEN
 PEAS, THAWED BUT NOT
 COOKED
⅔ CUP DRY ROASTED PEANUTS
 WITHOUT HULLS

1. Combine the sour cream, mayonnaise, Worcestershire sauce and curry powder.

2. Drain the peas thoroughly and mix them with the peanuts.

3. Pour the sour cream mixture over the pea mixture and mix them gently but completely. Serve cold.

SPINACH AND BACON SALAD

Jane Moulton

6 to 8 servings

1 10-OUNCE PACKAGE FRESH
 SPINACH
½ CUP MAYONNAISE
1 TEASPOON WORCESTERSHIRE
 SAUCE
½ TEASPOON GARLIC SALT
2 TABLESPOONS MINCED DRIED
 ONION
3 SLICES THICK BACON, COOKED
 CRISP AND CRUMBLED
3 HARD-COOKED EGGS, PEELED
 AND SLICED

1. Wash and thoroughly dry the spinach. Cut off any tough stems.

2. In a large salad bowl, combine all the remaining ingredients and mix well.

3. Tear the spinach and place it in a salad bowl; toss to mix well. Refrigerate until serving time. This salad stands up well for several hours.

KOREAN SPINACH SALAD

Paula J. Buchholz

6 to 8 servings

1 POUND FRESH SPINACH OR
  KALE, WELL WASHED AND DRIED
½ POUND BACON, COOKED UNTIL
  CRISP, DRAINED AND CRUMBLED
4 EGGS, HARD-COOKED AND DICED
½ POUND FRESH BEAN SPROUTS
1 CUP SALAD OIL
½ CUP SUGAR
⅓ CUP CATSUP

1 MEDIUM-SIZED ONION, COARSELY
  CHOPPED
¼ CUP VINEGAR
1 TABLESPOON WORCESTERSHIRE
  SAUCE
SALT TO TASTE
FRESHLY GROUND BLACK PEPPER
  TO TASTE

1. Tear the spinach into small pieces and place them in a salad bowl with the bacon, hard-cooked eggs and bean sprouts.

2. Place the remaining ingredients in the container of a blender or food processor and process until smooth.

3. Pour the dressing over the spinach and toss until each piece is well coated.

Legume and Rice Salads

ITALIAN SUMMER RICE SALAD
(INSALATA DI RISO)

Giuliano Bugialli

6 servings

Cold rice salads are extremely popular as summer dishes in Italy. This one takes advantage of the fresh vegetables and herbs of the season, set off by a light dressing.

1 POUND RAW RICE (PREFERABLY ITALIAN ARBORIO RICE, IF AVAILABLE)
SALT
1 LEMON
3 VERY SMALL ZUCCHINI
1 SMALL EGGPLANT
4 TABLESPOONS OLIVE OIL
1 GREEN PEPPER
1 VERY SMALL CUCUMBER
1 LARGE RIPE (BUT NOT OVER-RIPE) TOMATO

BLACK PEPPER
5 LARGE LEAVES FRESH BASIL

Sauce:
1 CLOVE GARLIC
1 LEMON
¼ CUP OLIVE OIL
SALT TO TASTE
FRESHLY GROUND BLACK PEPPER TO TASTE

1. Add the rice to a large quantity of salted boiling water and cook for about 20 minutes, until it is tender but firm (*al dente*).

2. Drain and cool the rice under cold running water and place it on a large serving dish.

3. Squeeze the lemon and pour the juice over the rice. Mix well with a wooden spoon.

4. Clean the zucchini and cut them into 1-inch pieces. Boil the pieces in salted water for about 3 minutes—or until they are cooked through but still crisp—then drain them and place them on a plate until cold.

5. Cut the eggplant into 1-inch squares. Pour the olive oil into a small saucepan and set it over medium heat. When the oil is hot, add the eggplant pieces. Sprinkle them with a little salt. Sauté the eggplant until soft, about 20 minutes, stirring every so often with a wooden spoon. Remove the eggplant from the pan and let it cool in a small bowl.

6. Loosen the skin of the green pepper on all sides by leaning it against a pot of water boiling on the stove, turning so that the skin blisters. When the skin

is loose, remove it as well as the seeds and interior membranes under cold running water. Cut the pepper into strips. Add the strips to the rice without mixing.

7. Slice the cucumber into thin slices and add to the serving dish.

8. Cut the tomato into 1-inch squares and place them on the serving dish.

9. To prepare the sauce, peel the clove of garlic, rub a small crockery bowl with it and discard the clove. Squeeze the lemon and add its juice to the bowl, along with the oil, salt and pepper. Mix well with a wooden spoon.

10. Place the cold zucchini and eggplant on the serving dish. Pour the sauce over the vegetables and rice. Mix gently but very well.

11. Tear the basil leaves into 2 or 3 pieces and sprinkle them over the salad.

RICE AND PORK SALAD
WITH ORANGES AND RED ONIONS

Elizabeth Colchie

4 servings

1½ TABLESPOONS DIJON-STYLE MUSTARD
1 TEASPOON SALT
2 TABLESPOONS LEMON JUICE
2 TABLESPOONS ORANGE JUICE
½ CUP OLIVE OIL
TABASCO OR HOT SAUCE TO TASTE
2½ CUPS COOKED, THINLY SLIVERED PORK LOIN

¼ CUP MINCED PARSLEY
3 CUPS COOKED RICE (STILL WARM, PREFERABLY)
2 TO 3 ORANGES, PEELED AND SECTIONED
1 SMALL RED ONION, VERY THINLY SLICED
1 BUNCH WATERCRESS, WASHED AND TRIMMED

1. In a jar combine the mustard, salt, lemon and orange juice and stir. Add the olive oil and shake to blend. Add Tabasco or hot sauce to taste.

2. Toss with the pork and let it marinate at least 30 minutes.

3. Add the parsley and rice and toss. Taste for seasoning. Refrigerate the mixture for several hours or overnight, covered.

4. Toss the rice gently with the oranges and onions. Mound the salad on a serving dish and surround with the watercress. Let the salad warm up slightly before serving.

LENTIL SALAD

Michael Batterberry

Michael Batterberry

12 to 16 servings

1 POUND LENTILS
2 CARROTS, SCRAPED
2 BAY LEAVES
1 TEASPOON THYME
1 TABLESPOON COARSE SALT,
  PLUS 1½ TEASPOONS
6 TABLESPOONS GOOD OLIVE OIL,
  PLUS 1 TABLESPOON
1½ TEASPOONS DRY MUSTARD
6 GRINDINGS OF BLACK PEPPER
1 TEASPOON GROUND CORIANDER
1 CLOVE GARLIC, CRUSHED

2 TABLESPOONS RED WINE
  VINEGAR
½ MEDIUM-SIZED RED ONION,
  FINELY CHOPPED
1 CUP CHOPPED CELERY
½ MEDIUM-SIZED RED ONION,
  SLICED PAPER THIN
1 TABLESPOON LEMON JUICE
⅔ CUP CHOPPED PARSLEY
GREEK BLACK OLIVES (OPTIONAL)
CAPERS (OPTIONAL)

1. Cook the lentils in water (to cover by at least 1½ inches) along with the carrots, bay leaves and thyme. When tender, but not at all mushy, season with 1 tablespoon of the salt, cook 1 minute more and drain in a colander. Remove the carrots and reserve them. Cooking time will vary anywhere from 18 to 25 minutes.

2. While the thoroughly-drained lentils are still warm, toss them in a dressing made by mixing 6 tablespoons of the olive oil into a paste with the dry mustard, the remaining salt, pepper, coriander, garlic and vinegar. Be careful not to mash the lentils. At the same time, dice the reserved carrots and stir them, the chopped onion and the celery into the lentils.

3. Let the mixture marinate at room temperature for at least 2 hours. Taste and correct the seasonings; more salt and pepper may be desired.

4. Mound the lentils into a low dome on a plate or platter and decorate with the onion rings (well rinsed under cold running water, paper-towel dried, and dressed with the lemon juice) and the chopped parsley. Greek black olives and capers are also extremely compatible as additional garnishes. This recipe may be halved.

SPICY SOY BEAN SALAD

Elizabeth Colchie

Elizabeth Colchie

6 servings

1 POUND DRIED SOY BEANS

1. Soy beans need lengthy soaking and cooking times. To prepare them, soak 1 pound of dried beans overnight in water to cover by about 4 inches. Drain, rinse, and pour them into a heavy saucepan with water to cover by 2 inches. Add 2 teaspoons of salt. Simmer, partly covered, for 3 hours, or until tender

(this will vary depending upon the age and state of dehydration of the beans, but don't worry, it is virtually impossible to overcook soy beans).

¾ CUP DICED SWEET RED PEPPER
¾ CUP DICED GREEN BELL
   PEPPER
½ CUP OLIVE OIL
1 CLOVE GARLIC, MINCED
1 TABLESPOON GROUND CUMIN
1 TEASPOON MINCED CANNED
   GREEN CHILI (OR MORE TO
   TASTE)
2 CUPS SLICED SCALLIONS

6 CUPS COOKED SOY BEANS
½ POUND *FETA* OR *BRYNDZA*
   CHEESE, CUT IN ½-INCH DICE
¼ CUP PITTED, SLICED OIL-CURED
   BLACK OLIVES
1 TO 2 TABLESPOONS LEMON
   JUICE
MINCED PARSLEY TO TASTE
BLACK PEPPER

1. In a large skillet, sauté the peppers in olive oil for 5 minutes.

2. Add the garlic, cumin, and minced chili and sauté for a few minutes to blend the flavors.

3. Add the scallions and toss a moment to soften.

4. Add the soy beans and stir until they are heated through.

5. Add the *feta* (or *bryndza*) and olives and stir 2 to 3 minutes, or until the cheese softens slightly.

6. Add the lemon juice, parsley and a generous amount of black pepper.

SUMMER RICE SALAD

Florence Fabricant

8 servings

3 CUPS WATER
SALT
1½ CUPS LONG-GRAIN RICE
1 CUP CHOPPED ONION
½ CUP OLIVE OIL
2 CUPS PEELED, SEEDED, CHOPPED
   RIPE TOMATOES
½ CUP CHOPPED GREEN PEPPER
½ CUP MAYONNAISE

3 TABLESPOONS VINEGAR
SALT TO TASTE
FRESHLY GROUND BLACK PEPPER
   TO TASTE
2 TABLESPOONS FRESH MINCED
   HERBS: PARSLEY, BASIL, CHIVES,
   ETC.
2 TABLESPOONS DRAINED CAPERS

1. Bring salted water to a boil in a heavy saucepan, add the rice, cover and simmer until the rice is tender, about 15 minutes.

2. Meanwhile, combine the onions and olive oil in a small pan and cook over medium heat until the onion is translucent.

3. When the rice is cooked, fold the onion and oil mixture into it. Fold in the tomatoes and green pepper. Allow to cool to room temperature.

4. Mix the mayonnaise and vinegar together and fold them into the rice mixture. Season to taste with salt and pepper, add the herbs and capers and chill before serving.

Seafood Salads

FRANÇOIS' CRAB AND AVOCADO SALAD

Harvey Steiman

4 servings

2 AVOCADOS
½ CUP MAYONNAISE
1 TEASPOON TOMATO CATSUP
10 OUNCES ALASKAN KING
  CRABMEAT
2 HARD-COOKED EGGS, ROUGHLY
  CHOPPED
1½ TABLESPOONS VODKA

1. Halve the avocados. Discard the seed and scoop out the flesh, leaving ½ to ¾ inch of flesh as a shell in the avocado skin. Slice the scooped-out flesh.

2. Combine the mayonnaise with the catsup and add to the crabmeat, tossing to coat it. Add the eggs and sliced avocado, toss well and heap into the avocado shells.

3. Just before serving, sprinkle with vodka.

APPETIZER EGG SALAD WITH SEAFOOD DRESSING

Ruth Ellen Church

6 servings

BIBB LETTUCE OR OTHER GREENS
6 HARD-COOKED EGGS
6 SLICES TOMATO

Dressing:
1 CUP MAYONNAISE
½ CUP CHILI SAUCE
4 GREEN ONIONS, MINCED
½ TEASPOON SALT

1 TEASPOON WORCESTERSHIRE
  SAUCE
1 CAN (6½ TO 7 OUNCES) TUNA
  OR 1 CUP COOKED OR CANNED
  SHRIMP OR CRAB

Garnish:
GREEN OR RIPE OLIVES

38

1. Arrange the greens on chilled plates. Cut the chilled eggs lengthwise in half, then cut each half into three sections. Arrange the sections of one egg on a tomato slice on each plate.

2. Combine the dressing ingredients and add them to the salad, or serve the dressing separately. Garnish with olives.

SHRIMP WITH MELON IN KIRSCH

Ruth Spear

4 servings

This recipe is an old European one that originally called for lobster instead of shrimp. A friend began making it with shrimp in the days when the price difference between the two was significant. We liked it so much we have been eating it that way ever since, usually as a first course in the summer.

20 MEDIUM-SIZED SHRIMP,
   COOKED, PEELED AND DEVEINED
½ MEDIUM-SIZED RIPE MELON,
   SPANISH, CASABA OR HONEYDEW
2 INSIDE STALKS CELERY, DICED
1 CUP MAYONNAISE, PREFERABLY
   HOMEMADE
1 TABLESPOON CHILI SAUCE
¼ TEASPOON TABASCO OR HOT
   SAUCE
2 TABLESPOONS KIRSCH
SALT

1. Cut the shrimp cross-wise into 3 pieces each.

2. Cut the melon into cubes of a size compatible with the shrimp. Drain off as much of the melon juice as you can and reserve it in a cup.

3. Combine the shrimp and melon with the celery in a bowl and set it aside.

4. Put the mayonnaise in a small bowl. Beat in the chili sauce, the Tabasco, the kirsch, and salt to taste. Thin the sauce to a pleasing consistency with some of the reserved melon juice.

5. Pour the sauce over the shrimp mixture, cover it, and allow to mellow at least 1 hour in the refrigerator.

FISHERMAN'S SALAD
(INSALATA PESCATORE)

Nicola Zanghi

4 servings

Dressing:
⅔ CUP OLIVE OIL
⅓ CUP LEMON JUICE
1 EGG YOLK
1 TEASPOON DIJON-STYLE
   MUSTARD
2 CLOVES GARLIC, CRUSHED
1 TEASPOON SALT
1 TEASPOON WORCESTERSHIRE
   SAUCE
¼ TEASPOON OREGANO

Other Ingredients:
½ HEAD ROMAINE, WELL WASHED

½ HEAD CHICORY, WELL WASHED
1½ POUNDS COLD POACHED OR
   STEAMED FISH OR SHELLFISH
   SUCH AS BASS, SNAPPER, FRESH
   TUNA, SQUID, SCALLOPS, SHRIMP,
   CRABMEAT, MUSSELS, LOBSTER
   MEAT, OR SALMON OR A
   COMBINATION OF SEVERAL
   COLD FISH
3 TABLESPOONS CHOPPED
   PARSLEY
WATERCRESS FOR GARNISH
FRESHLY GROUND PEPPER

1. Whisk together all of the ingredients for the dressing one day in advance. Remove the garlic cloves before serving.

2. Shred or tear apart the chicory and romaine. Place on a serving platter.

3. Place the fish, chopped parsley and watercress on top of the greens. Pour the dressing over the salad and pepper generously. Serve.

SCALLOP, MUSHROOM AND CELERY SALAD

Nan Mabon

4 servings

½ POUND SEA SCALLOPS
½ POUND VERY FRESH
   MUSHROOMS
4 RIBS CELERY
1 TABLESPOON FINELY CHOPPED
   PARSLEY
JUICE OF 1 LEMON
SALT TO TASTE
FRESHLY GROUND BLACK PEPPER
   TO TASTE
5 TABLESPOONS OLIVE OIL

1. Slice the raw scallops into thin pieces, then plunge them into a small pot of boiling water. Immediately remove the pot from the heat and stir the scallops until they lose their translucent look and turn white (about 30 to 60 seconds). Drain and rinse them under cold water.

2. With a damp paper towel, wipe off any dirt that clings to the mushrooms. Trim off the tips of the stems, then slice the mushrooms thin. Wash the celery, wipe it dry and slice it.

3. Put the scallops, mushrooms, celery and parsley in a serving bowl. Pour on the lemon juice, add the salt, pepper and olive oil. Toss and allow to sit 10 minutes before serving.

SALADE NIÇOISE

Joanne Will

6 servings

Dressing:
¾ CUP OLIVE OIL
¼ CUP RED WINE VINEGAR
1 SMALL ONION, THINLY SLICED
2 TABLESPOONS MINCED PARSLEY
6 ANCHOVY FILLETS, CHOPPED
¼ TEASPOON SALT

Other Ingredients:
4 MEDIUM-SIZED POTATOES, COOKED AND DICED

1 CUP COOKED GREEN BEANS
1 CUP GREEK OR ITALIAN BLACK OLIVES
CRISP SALAD GREENS
1 TABLESPOON CAPERS
1 LARGE TOMATO, CUT IN WEDGES
2 HARD-COOKED EGGS, CUT IN WEDGES
1 CAN (6½ TO 7 OUNCES) WHITE TUNA, DRAINED AND CHILLED

1. Combine the oil, vinegar, onion, parsley, anchovies, and salt; mix until blended.

2. Mix the potatoes, beans, and olives in a bowl and toss gently with some of the dressing to blend. Let stand 15 to 30 minutes at room temperature.

3. Line a platter or salad bowl with crisp greens. With a slotted spoon, transfer the potato mixture to the center of the platter. Pour off any excess dressing and add it to the remaining dressing in a sauceboat.

4. Sprinkle the capers over the potato mixture. Arrange the tomato wedges, egg wedges, and tuna chunks around the mound of potato salad. Pass the sauceboat of dressing.

Meat, Poultry, and Cheese Salads

BEEF AND GREEN BEAN SALAD
(SALAD ARGENTINE)

Maurice Moore-Betty

4 servings

1½ POUNDS GREEN BEANS
2 TABLESPOONS SALT
2 POUNDS ROAST BEEF SLICED
AND CUT INTO MATCHSTICK
STRIPS
3 TABLESPOONS FINELY CHOPPED
PARSLEY

6 TABLESPOONS OLIVE OR
SALAD OIL
2 TEASPOONS LEMON JUICE
½ TEASPOON SALT
2 TABLESPOONS DIJON-STYLE
MUSTARD
4 TABLESPOONS SOUR CREAM
FRESHLY GROUND BLACK PEPPER

Dressing:
1½ TABLESPOONS RED WINE
VINEGAR

1. Bring fresh water to a rolling boil in a 3-quart pan. Cut off the tops and tails of the beans with a pair of scissors, dropping them into a bowl of very cold water as they are trimmed.

2. When the beans are ready, add the salt to the boiling water. Toss in the beans by the handful, attempting to keep the water at the boil. Cook for 4 minutes after the last of the beans has been added and the water has again come to the boil. They should be 'al dente', still crisp.

3. Plunge the beans into a large bowl of cold water to stop the cooking, drain them, and set them aside.

4. Mix all the dressing ingredients in a small bowl. Cover the beans and strips of beef with enough dressing to coat generously. Sprinkle with parsley and heap into a salad bowl.

CHINESE CHICKEN SALAD

Carole Lalli

4 servings

2 LARGE OR 3 SMALL CHICKEN
  BREASTS
2 CUPS CHICKEN STOCK
4 SLICES FRESH GINGER
3 SCALLIONS
1 TABLESPOON SOY SAUCE
¼ POUND FRESH BEAN SPROUTS
2 TABLESPOONS TOASTED SESAME
  SEEDS
BOSTON LETTUCE LEAVES

Dressing:
2 TABLESPOONS SOY SAUCE
1 TABLESPOON SESAME OIL
1 TABLESPOON CHINESE VINEGAR
  OR RICE WINE VINEGAR
1 TEASPOON CHINESE MUSTARD
  DISSOLVED IN 1 TEASPOON
  WATER

1. Poach the chicken in the stock with the ginger, 2 of the scallions, roughly chopped, and a generous dash of soy sauce, until the chicken turns white all the way through. Remove the pan from the heat and let the chicken cool in the broth.

2. When the chicken is cool, shred it by hand; combine it with the bean sprouts and remaining scallion (the white part and about 2 inches of the green cut into fine matchstick slivers).

3. Combine the ingredients for the dressing.

4. Toss the mixture thoroughly with the dressing and sprinkle it with sesame seeds. Scoop onto Boston lettuce leaves.

SUMMER FRUIT AND DUCKLING SALAD

Emanuel and Madeline Greenberg

4 servings

3 LARGE RIPE PEACHES, PEELED
  AND CUBED
JUICE OF 1 LARGE LEMON
2 CUPS CUBED COOKED DUCK
2 MEDIUM-SIZED SEEDLESS
  ORANGES, PEELED AND
  SECTIONED
½ MEDIUM-SIZED RED ONION,
  THINLY SLICED AND SEPARATED
  INTO RINGS

¼ CUP SLICED PITTED BLACK
  OLIVES
¼ CUP ORANGE JUICE
¾ CUP SALAD OIL
1 TABLESPOON CHOPPED ONION
2 SPRIGS PARSLEY
1 TEASPOON SOY SAUCE
½ TEASPOON DRIED TARRAGON
SALT TO TASTE
PEPPER TO TASTE

1. Toss the peach cubes, with 1 tablespoon of the lemon juice, in a salad bowl.

2. Add the duck, orange sections, onion rings and olives.

3. Combine the remaining lemon juice with the rest of the ingredients in a blender. Whirl smooth. Pour over the salad; mix gently.

GREEK VILLAGE SALAD WITH FETA CHEESE
(HORIATIKI SALATA)

Vilma Liacouras Chantiles

Vilma Liacouras Chantiles

4 servings

Originating in the provinces and islands where the ingredients are plentiful, this salad is casually mixed, colorful and nutritious. The *feta* is salty. Add salt and oil sparingly and vinegar liberally!

1 CLOVE GARLIC, CUT IN HALF (OPTIONAL)
5 RIPE, FIRM TOMATOES OF GOOD FLAVOR, QUARTERED
2 MEDIUM-SIZED GREEN PEPPERS, SLICED OR CHOPPED
4 SCALLIONS, CHOPPED, OR 1 LARGE ONION, SLICED OR CHOPPED
2 FIRM CUCUMBERS, LARGE SEEDS REMOVED, CUT INTO CHUNKS

12 TO 14 GREEK OLIVES
1 CUP *FETA* CHEESE, BROKEN OR CUT INTO FINGER-TIP PIECES
2 TO 3 TABLESPOONS FINE OLIVE OIL
3 TO 4 TABLESPOONS RED WINE VINEGAR
SALT (OPTIONAL)
FRESHLY GROUND BLACK PEPPER
DRIED OREGANO, PREFERABLY GREEK OR ITALIAN

1. If using garlic, rub your salad bowl with the cut end.

2. Toss the garlic with the tomatoes, peppers, scallions (or onion), cucumbers, olives and *feta*. Remove the garlic clove.

3. Season with olive oil and vinegar, sparingly with salt, and add black pepper.

4. Crumble the oregano; sprinkle it over the salad.

Note: Another delicious version for the dressing: Mash a chunk of *feta* with a fork, add oil and vinegar to the *feta* and dribble over the salad.

CHICKEN, POTATO AND TOMATO SALAD
WITH BASIL MAYONNAISE

Elizabeth Colchie

Elizabeth Colchie

6 servings

1 3-TO-4 POUND CHICKEN, FRESHLY ROASTED AND COMPLETELY COOLED
3 TO 4 CUPS FRESHLY COOKED, PEELED NEW POTATOES (COOKED IN THEIR JACKETS, THEN PEELED), COOLED
FRESH BASIL

OLIVE OIL
⅔ CUP MAYONNAISE, CHILLED (PREFERABLY HOMEMADE)
SALT
PEPPER
LEMON JUICE
4 RIPE TOMATOES

1. Remove the chicken skin and cut the meat into 1-inch pieces; cut the potatoes into 1-inch cubes; place both in a large bowl.

44

2. In the container of a blender, purée enough basil with a very small amount of olive oil to make about 3 tablespoons of basil paste (or use 3 tablespoons of *pesto*); mix into the mayonnaise.

3. Add the mayonnaise mixture to the chicken and potatoes and toss lightly; season with salt, pepper and lemon juice.

4. Slice the tomatoes and arrange them around a serving dish. Spoon the salad into the center and serve.

SESAME CHICKEN SALAD
(PON PON CHICKEN)

Michael Tong

6 to 12 appetizer servings

2 CUPS STEAMED, BOILED OR GENTLY SIMMERED CHICKEN, SHREDDED
LETTUCE LEAVES TO COVER SERVING PLATTER
1 TABLESPOON CHOPPED SCALLION
1 TEASPOON OR MORE CHOPPED GARLIC
1½ TEASPOONS FINELY CHOPPED GINGER
3 TABLESPOONS WELL-STIRRED SESAME PASTE*

1½ TABLESPOONS SOY SAUCE, PREFERABLY DARK
1 TABLESPOON WHITE VINEGAR, PREFERABLY RICE VINEGAR
1 TEASPOON SUGAR
1 TEASPOON MONOSODIUM GLUTAMATE (OPTIONAL)
SALT TO TASTE
1 TABLESPOON CHILI PASTE WITH GARLIC*
1 TABLESPOON SESAME OIL*

1. Place the chicken on the lettuce leaves, arranged on a serving dish.

2. Blend the remaining ingredients and pour the sauce over the chicken.

 * These ingredients are available in Oriental groceries.

SWISS-STYLE CHEESE SALAD

Ruth Ellen Church

6 servings

1 POUND SWISS OR GRUYÈRE
CHEESE, CUT IN SMALL DICE
2 TABLESPOONS MINCED PARSLEY
2 TABLESPOONS MINCED CHIVES
¼ CUP FINELY CUT GREEN PEPPER
½ CUP CHOPPED CELERY
2 HARD-COOKED EGGS, DICED
½ CUP CUBED HAM, SUMMER
SAUSAGE OR LEBANON
BOLOGNA

½ CUP MAYONNAISE
1 TABLESPOON DIJON-STYLE
MUSTARD
1½ TEASPOONS WHITE WINE
VINEGAR
SALT
PEPPER
LETTUCE, OR OTHER GREENS

1. In a bowl, place the cheese, parsley, chives, green pepper, celery, eggs, and meat.

2. Mix the mayonnaise, mustard and vinegar and blend with the other ingredients, adding more mayonnaise if you wish, and salt and pepper if needed.

3. Line another bowl with greens, fill it with the salad and keep cold until served.

Fruit Salads

MELON, CUCUMBER AND TOMATO SALAD WITH HERBED BREAD

Nathalie Dupree

6 servings

French dressing:
½ CUP LEMON JUICE
¾ CUP OIL
½ TEASPOON DRY MUSTARD
2 TEASPOONS SALT
PEPPER
1 TEASPOON SUGAR
1 TABLESPOON CHOPPED PARSLEY
1 TABLESPOON CHOPPED MINT
1 TABLESPOON CHOPPED CHIVES

Other Ingredients:
1 CUCUMBER
SALT
1 MELON (CANTALOUPE OR HONEYDEW)
1 POUND FRESH RED TOMATOES
1 LOAF FRENCH BREAD
8 TABLESPOONS (1 STICK) BUTTER, SOFTENED
4 TABLESPOONS FRESH CHOPPED HERBS

1. Mix the French dressing.

2. Cut the cucumber into cubes, salt them lightly and let them stand while preparing the rest of the salad.

3. Quarter the melon, seed it, then carefully slice the melon from the rind, leaving the rind intact.

4. Cut the melon into balls or cubes.

5. Skin and quarter the tomatoes and remove the seeds.

6. Rinse the cucumber and dry it.

7. Mix the melon, cucumber and tomatoes together; moisten with the dressing and herbs. Chill.

8. Arrange the melon rind shells on end against the sides of a bowl to form a "tulip." Fill the bowl with the fruit.

9. To prepare the herb bread, mix the herbs into the softened butter.

10. Cut a loaf of French bread into ½-inch-thick slices. Spread the slices with herb butter, reassemble, and then cover the whole top of the loaf with butter. Wrap the bread in foil and bake in a moderate oven until warm. Serve with the salad.

GRAPEFRUIT, CELERY AND PEPPER SALAD

Maurice Moore-Betty

4 to 6 servings

4 SEEDLESS GRAPEFRUIT
6 RIBS CELERY
1 GREEN BELL PEPPER
1 RED BELL PEPPER
½ CUP PARSLEY SPRIGS
¼ CUP OLIVE OIL
SALT TO TASTE
PEPPER TO TASTE
LETTUCE LEAVES

1. Peel the grapefruit and section each one into a colander standing in a mixing bowl.

2. Scrape the celery ribs with a vegetable peeler to remove the stringy fibers. Cut them on the bias into ⅛-inch-thick slices.

3. Halve and quarter the peppers, removing all pith and seeds. Slice the peppers the same thickness as the celery.

4. Chop the parsley.

5. In a large mixing bowl, mix the grapefruit, celery, peppers and parsley. (Save the grapefruit juice that will have drained into the bowl for breakfast.)

6. Add the ¼ cup olive oil and salt and pepper to taste. Serve on a bed of lettuce.

APPLE-GRAPE "SALADE ALICE"

Raymond Sokolov

6 servings

6 LARGE, RIPE EATING APPLES
  WITH STEMS
1 LEMON
1⅓ CUPS RED GRAPES, HALVED
  AND SEEDED
1⅓ CUPS WALNUTS OR BLANCHED
  ALMONDS, ROUGHLY CHOPPED
½ CUP HEAVY CREAM
  (APPROXIMATELY)
SALT
3 LETTUCE HEARTS, WASHED,
  DRIED AND HALVED

1. Slice the tops off the apples, taking care to leave the stems intact. Rub the exposed flesh with the lemon. Set the apples aside, and reserve the lemon.

2. Cut away the remaining flesh from the insides of the apples, leaving only enough so that thin, free-standing shells remain. Rub the inner walls of these shells with the lemon.

3. Discard the cores and seeds of the apple and dice the remaining flesh. Pour water into one of the apples and then into a measuring cup. Note the level of the water and then discard it. Measure out twice this amount of diced apple and combine it with equal amounts of grapes and nuts.

4. Just before serving, squeeze as much juice as you can out of the reserved lemon and combine it with the heavy cream. Add salt to taste, and then stir gradually into the fruit mixture. Add more cream, if needed, to coat the salad completely.

5. Fill the apple shells with the salad. Put the tops back on the apples and arrange them on a serving platter, alternating with the lettuce hearts.

PEAR SALAD WITH CHUTNEY FRENCH DRESSING

Joanne Will

4 servings

Dressing:
½ CUP SALAD OR OLIVE OIL
¼ CUP WHITE WINE VINEGAR
1 SMALL ONION, SLICED
1 TEASPOON DIJON-STYLE
   MUSTARD
¾ TEASPOON SALT
⅛ TEASPOON PEPPER
¼ CUP MANGO CHUTNEY
1 TABLESPOON CHILI SAUCE

Other Ingredients:
2 LARGE RIPE PEARS
2 BUNCHES FRESH WATERCRESS

1. To make the dressing, put the oil, vinegar, onion, mustard, salt, and pepper in a blender container. Blend the ingredients until smooth.

2. Add the chutney and chili sauce. Flick the blender on and off several times, until the chutney is coarsely chopped. Put the dressing in a covered glass jar. Chill to blend the flavors. Makes about 1 cup.

3. Peel, halve, and core the pears. Arrange a pear half, cut side down, on a bed of watercress, on a chilled salad plate. Drizzle with dressing.

Note: Any leftover dressing can be used on other fruit salads. It's also good on cold chicken or shrimp.

WATERMELON FRUIT BASKET
WITH ORANGE-LEMON DRESSING

Nathalie Dupree

12 to 15 servings

1 LARGE OVAL WATERMELON THAT WILL SIT EVENLY ON ONE SIDE. (CUT OFF A THIN SLICE, IF NECESSARY.)

3 TO 4 QUARTS OF SMALL PIECES OF FRUIT: A COMBINATION OF 1 QUART OF WATERMELON, CANTALOUPE OR HONEYDEW MELON, STRAWBERRIES AND RASPBERRIES, SLICED PEACHES, SLICED PEARS, PINEAPPLE AND/ OR SEEDED GRAPES (OR WHAT-EVER VARIETY OF FRUIT YOU CAN GET FRESH)

Dressing:
⅔ CUP FRESH ORANGE JUICE
¼ CUP FRESH LEMON JUICE
½ CUP SUGAR
SALT
4 EGG YOLKS, LIGHTLY BEATEN
1½ CUPS WHIPPED CREAM
GRATED ORANGE PEEL (ENOUGH TO SPRINKLE ON TOP OF THE BASKET)

1. Make a basket from the watermelon, cutting in from the long ends, taking care to leave a "handle" spanning the center. You may cut the edges into either a scalloped or a serrated pattern.

2. Take out the heart from the melon and leave just a small portion of the pink on the bottom and sides to form a bed for the fruit. The heart may be scooped into small balls or cut into bite-sized pieces. (Use as part of the 3 to 4 quarts of fruit, above.)

3. Drain the watermelon basket. Be careful not to damage the handle. Chill it as long as possible; several hours is preferable.

4. To make the dressing, in a small saucepan combine the orange and lemon juices, sugar and salt and place over low heat.

5. When the sugar is melted, bring the syrup to a simmer for a moment or two.

6. Make a *bain marie* from another, larger pan, such as a frying pan. Pour water into the frying pan and place the pan containing the syrup in it.

7. Gradually add the slightly beaten egg yolks, whisking constantly. Do not let the mixture boil, but cook and stir over the *bain marie* until the mixture is smooth and thick. Chill.

8. Fold the whipped cream into the dressing, then fold the dressing into the fruit.

9. Fill the shell with the chilled fruit and sprinkle the grated orange peel on top.

Note: I confess that I serve this dressing not only on watermelon but also on a salad of oranges and red lettuce, on chilled asparagus, and a number of other things. Without the whipped cream, it can be served as a hot sauce.

HONEY-LIME POPPY SEED DRESSING
WITH FRUIT

Lyn Stallworth

6 to 8 servings

This fruit salad is a fine complement to barbecued steak, hamburgers or chicken.

¼ CUP WHITE VINEGAR
¼ CUP FRESH LIME JUICE
1 TEASPOON DRY MUSTARD
1 TEASPOON GRATED ONION
¼ CUP SUGAR
¼ CUP HONEY
1 CUP VEGETABLE OIL
¼ TEASPOON SALT
2 TABLESPOONS POPPY SEEDS
¼ CUP BOURBON WHISKEY

Dressing (1½ cups):
1. In a small enameled saucepan, whisk the vinegar and lime juice with the dry mustard to dissolve any lumps. Add the grated onion, sugar, honey, vegetable oil and salt. Whisk the mixture over moderate heat until it boils; simmer for a minute so that the sugar and salt dissolve.

2. Remove the dressing from the heat and add the poppy seeds and Bourbon.

3. Cool the dressing to room temperature before serving it, or cover it tightly with plastic wrap and refrigerate it. In that case, return it to room temperature before using it, and stir it well.

Fruit Salad Suggestions:
Combinations of any of the following fresh fruits would be excellent with the dressing: sliced peaches and apricots, cubed pineapple, sliced avocado, grapefruit and orange sections, sliced bananas, seedless grapes, melon balls, ripe papaya, kiwi or mango slices.

1. Arrange the prepared fruit in a wide shallow bowl; spoon some of the dressing over it and pass additional dressing in a sauceboat. Or arrange the fruit on individual plates.

   Note: For the 1½ cups of dressing, you will need about 2½ quarts of fruit. However, if you want to serve smaller salads, the dressing can be kept safely for 6 to 8 days, refrigerated and covered with plastic wrap.

EDITORS

Arnold Goldman
Barbara Spiegel
Lyn Stallworth

EDITORIAL ASSISTANT

Christopher Carter

EDITORIAL CONSULTANTS

Wendy Afton Rieder
Kate Slate

CONTRIBUTORS

Introduction by Lyn Stallworth

Michael Batterberry, author of several books on food, art and social history, is also a painter, and is editor and food critic for a number of national magazines. He has taught at James Beard's cooking classes in New York and many of his original recipes have appeared in *House & Garden, House Beautiful* and *Harper's Bazaar.*

Paula J. Buchholz is the regional co-ordinator for the National Culinary Apprenticeship Program. She has been a food writer for the *Detroit Free Press* and for the *San Francisco Examiner.*

Giuliano Bugialli, author of *The Fine Art of Italian Cooking,* is co-founder and teacher of Cooking in Florence, a program conducted in Italy. He also has a cooking school in New York.

Vilma Liacouras Chantiles, author of *The Food of Greece,* writes a food and consumer column for the *Scarsdale* (New York) *Inquirer* and a monthly food column for the *Athenian Magazine* (Athens, Greece).

Grace Zia Chu, author of the extraordinarily successful *The Pleasures of Chinese Cooking* and, more recently, *Madame Chu's Chinese Cooking School,* has taught Chinese cooking both in her own school and at the China Institute of America in New York City.

Ruth Ellen Church, a syndicated wine columnist for the *Chicago Tribune,* had been food editor for that newspaper for more than thirty years when she recently retired. The author of seven cookbooks, her most recent book is *Entertaining with Wine.* Mrs. Church's *Wines and Cheeses of the Midwest* will be published in the fall of 1977.

Elizabeth Colchie is a noted food consultant who has done extensive recipe development and testing as well as research into the history of foods and cookery. She was on the editorial staff of *The Cooks' Catalogue* and has written numerous articles for such magazines as *Gourmet, House & Garden* and *Family Circle.*

Carol Cutler, who has been a food columnist for the *Washington Post,* is a graduate of the Cordon Bleu and L'Ecole des Trois Gourmands in Paris. She is the author of *Haute Cuisine for Your Heart's Delight,* and *The Six-Minute Soufflé and Other Culinary Delights.* She has also written for *House & Garden, American Home* and *Harper's Bazaar.*

Julie Dannenbaum is the founding director of the largest non-professional cooking school in the country, the Creative Cooking School in Philadelphia. She is the author of *Julie Dannenbaum's Creative Cooking School* and *Menus for All Occasions.* She is also Director of the Gritti Palace Hotel Cooking School in Venice and The Grand Hotel Cooking School in Rome.

Nathalie Dupree has been Director of Rich's Cooking School in Atlanta, Georgia, since it opened in September, 1975. She has an Advanced Certificate from the London Cordon Bleu and has owned restaurants in Spain and Georgia.

Florence Fabricant is a free-lance writer, reporting on restaurants and food for *The New York Times, New York* magazine and other publications. She was on the staff of *The Cooks' Catalogue* and editor of the paperback edition.

The Good Cooking School is an association of many of the world's authorities on the selection, preparation and serving of fine food and drink. Included are the owner-chefs of three-star restaurants of France, and eminent cookbook authors; food writers, editors, columnists; and teachers, lecturers and demonstrators specializing in information on food and wine. The association was formed in 1973.

Emanuel and Madeline Greenberg co-authored *Whiskey in the Kitchen* and are consultants to the food and beverage industry. Emanuel, a home economist, is a regular contributor to the food columns of *Playboy* magazine.

Diana Kennedy, the leading authority on the food of Mexico, is the author of *The Cuisines of Mexico* and *The Tortilla Book.*

Carole Lalli is a contributing editor to *New West* magazine and is its restaurant reviewer. She formerly ran a catering business in New York.

Jeanne Lesem, Family Editor of United Press International, is the author of *The Pleasures of Preserving and Pickling.*

Nan Mabon, a free-lance food writer and cooking teacher in New York City, is also cook for a private executive dining room on Wall Street. She studied at the Cordon Bleu in London.

Helen McCully is food editor of *House Beautiful* magazine and the author of many books on food, among them *Nobody Ever Tells You These Things About Food and Drink, Cooking with Helen McCully Beside You,* and most recently, *Waste Not, Want Not: A Cookbook of Delicious Foods from Leftovers.* She was a consultant on the staff of *The Cooks' Catalogue.*

Gloria Bley Miller is the author of *Learn Chinese Cooking in Your Own Kitchen* and *The Thousand Recipe Chinese Cookbook.*

Maurice Moore-Betty, owner-operator of The Civilized Art Cooking School, food consultant and restaurateur, is author of *Cooking for Occasions, The Maurice Moore-Betty Cooking School Book of Fine Cooking* and *The Civilized Art of Salad Making.*

Jane Moulton, a food writer for the *Plain Dealer* in Cleveland, took her degree in foods and nutrition. As well as reporting on culinary matters and reviewing food-related books for the *Plain Dealer,* she has worked in recipe development, public relations and catering.

Paul Rubinstein is the author of *Feasts for Two, The Night Before Cookbook* and *Feasts for Twelve (or More).* He is a stockbroker and the son of pianist Artur Rubinstein.

Raymond Sokolov, author of *The Saucier's Apprentice,* is a free-lance writer with a particular interest in food.

Ruth Spear is the author of the *East Hampton Cookbook* and writes occasional pieces on food for *New York* magazine. She is currently at work on a new cookbook.

Lyn Stallworth was associated with the Time-Life *Foods of the World* series and has written a food column for *Viva* magazine.

Harvey Steiman is food editor of the *Miami Heraid.* He has taught cooking classes and lectured on wine and restaurants at the Food and Hotel School of Florida International University.

Michael Tong is Managing Director of three of the finest Chinese restaurants in New York: Shun Lee Dynasty, Shun Lee Palace and Hunam.

Joanne Will is food editor of the *Chicago Tribune* and is a member of three Chicago wine and food societies.

Paula Wolfert, author of *Mediterranean Cooking* and *Couscous and Other Good Food from Morocco,* is also a cooking teacher and consultant. She has written articles for *Vogue* and other magazines.

Nicola Zanghi is the owner-chef of Restaurant Zanghi in Glen Cove, New York. He started his apprenticeship under his father at the age of thirteen, and is a graduate of two culinary colleges. He has been an instructor at the Cordon Bleu school in New York City.